MW01223400

ROADS AND REMINISCENCES

By

Linda Hughes-Dorame

ISBN: 1-4033-3453-6 (e-book)
ISBN: 1-4033-3454-4 (Paperback)

Library of Congress Control Number: 2002092186

This book is printed on acid free paper.

Printed in the United States of America
Bloomington, IN

1st Books - rev. 10/11/02

Dedication

Dedicated to the Memory of my Mom and Dad

**A Tribute to my Dad
in his Own Words**

Opportunities
by Frank R. Proctor (1908-1972)

What are opportunities?
How often do they come?
How can we prepare ourselves
to receive them?
What happens when we accept?
What happens if we reject?

Introduction

As I began compiling the material for this book, I thought about the words of Langston Hughes. "Life is a big sea full of many fish. I let down my nets and pull." I have pulled these poems, short stories, a play, and a speech together as I saw the opportunity had arrived. I was prepared to receive it.

The opportunity to share one's thoughts, ideas, and experiences with others is truly a gift to be treasured. I am sure the readers of this book will treasure the experience of reading this book and perhaps pull a fish that will somehow enhance their lives.

TABLE OF CONTENTS

POEMS BY LINDA HUGHES-DORAME, MARIA HUGHES-DORAME, AND FRANCES HENDERSON

Linda Hughes-Dorame

The Courage of Peter Salem

Listen my son and you shall hear
of a great man who knew no fear.
On June 17, 1775-
no one is now alive who remembers
that day and year.
The British forces in mockery
envisioned no difficulty
in defeating the American on Breed's Hill.
Little knew they of their loyalty and skill.
For as they were at near surrender
Peter Salem arose as the defender,
shooting the British major,
and what stunning behavior
that caused the Americans to retreat
and the British's ultimate defeat.
So hat's off to Peter, the man,
a freed slave from the colony
of Massachusetts's Flamingham.

Linda Hughes-Dorame

Linda Hughes-Dorame

Viva! El Cinco De Mayo

To My Husband

Viva! El Cinco de Mayo,
jewel of the State of Pueblo.
Forever crown its spirit that-
reigns as liberty's testament
and celebrates the victory won
by Mexico's courageous sons,
who defeated the formidable foe
on the gray morning of May 5th
at the great, swift, Battle of Pueblo.

Linda Hughes-Dorame

The Fulani Mask

Fulani mask on my living room wall
holding tales of history,
having traveled afar
from Nigeria, Chad, or Mali.
Did a dancer once wear you
With all your complexity?
Were you used to herald an event
or serve as a symbol of beauty?
Perhaps you spoke of a vital
moral or spiritual concern
and now stand tacked to my wall
as a lesson to learn.

Linda Hughes-Dorame

Dispossessed Farmer

He once owned this barren land
and fields of shining wheat grew
but where he went nobody knew.
The top of the hill where
the farmhouse set
now is deserted and desolate
and at the edge of the road
a sparkling stream
calls to tell of his dream.

Linda Hughes-Dorame

The Salt and Pepper Shakers

To my son and Daughter

At the center of the dining table
sits two salt and pepper shakers,
porcelain, bell-shaped, white and tan
with signed, imprinted, photographs
depicting past renowned marriage partners
of a highly acclaimed family clan,
President John F. Kennedy
and Mrs. John F. Kennedy.
As I glance at these keepsakes,
reminiscences slowly awake
of my late dad having purchased these
after the late President's fateful day
while silent words seem heard to say,
"Don't let it forgot,
the bells once tolled for Camelot."

Linda Hughes-Dorame

The Native American Dream Catcher

In Memory of my husband's Indian grandmother

Oh, dream catcher
hanging over my head
hold steadfast pleasant dreams
as I rest in bed.
But cast to the wind
all those that offend.

Linda Hughes-Dorame

The US Supreme Court Rule

In memory of Grandma Simpson and Topeka born,
Gwendolyn Brooks

The sun shone brightly that September day
over Topeka's plains as if it'd words to say,
And I as a child of age gour
viewed it from the classroom door.
While standing anxious and bright-eyed,
my dad and pal was at my side.
It was the very first day of school
after an infamous rule.
A great court battle had been won,
as Brown versed the Board of Education.
Now I'd be surprised to hear and see,
hope in mom and dad when they spoke to me
about this once forbidden school,
and the US Supreme Court rule.

Linda Hughes-Dorame

The Storm

I hear the ruthless wind
and see the relentless rain,
to energize sorrow, grief,
agony, and pain,
but the energy used to
fuel the storm
can also bring forth tranquil peace
and protection from harm.

Linda Hughes-Dorame

The Celtic Cross of Durrow

To my beautiful Irish/Hispanic Mother-in-law

Next to mirror on the wall hangs,
the Celtic Cross of Durrow
with the symbols of the number four,
to symbolize life's force to discipline
and man and woman to defend.
And reminiscent also to me
of the great matriarch, Mrs. Rose Kennedy
who passed from this life on a January 22nd
reuniting also with her loving dad,
who'd passed away on an October 2nd.
And I with a birthdate of October 22nd
will on day also reunite as well
with dear dad who passed one January 2nd
and with God, our father, forever dwell.

Linda Hughes-Dorame

Viva Zapata!

Viva Zapata!
Mexico's peasant's hero,
once a skilled horse trainer
for the rodeo.
Born in Mexico in 1879
of a poor Indigenous family
having heritage of Afro-Mexicans,
bravely would be give his life
for justice and fair distribution of land.
Yet forever will he give his life
on Mexican soil of Emiliano Zapata,
leader of Mexico's social revolution
and subscriber to the Place of Ayala.

Linda Hughes-Dorame

Our Son and Daughter

Afar across the sea
in the land of Germany,
we were blessed with
the birth of our most precious son.
Two years after
we'd crossed the water,
we were blessed,
with a beautiful daughter.

Linda Hughes-Dorame

Linda Hughes-Dorame

On Presenting Lorraine Hansberry's Play

To my daughter

The radiance of her light,
the zeal of her play,
"A Raisin in the Sun,"
Her young life of unfulfilled promise
ending almost as her work had begun,
all were so temporarily lent
as from the drama of Camelot
for one brief shining moment.
For one moment did her sun
illuminate the dried grapes of hope
of a poor southside Chicago family
while celebrating Africa's ancient majesty.
Yet forever did it enhance the lure
of America's dramatic theater.

Linda Hughes-Dorame

On   Reading   Emily Dickinson's Poem

It was a cool, clear, Oklahoma morn.
where aloud I read Enily Dickinson's poem.
The brisk, spring, morning air
seemed to usher me there-
to a girl at sea's edge with her dog.
standing on stage of sand in the bog.
The mermaids sprang from below
to watch the upcoming show
Suddenly she's rushed from the tidewater
by waves attempting to devour her.
Years have passed since that day-
still vividly the act replays,
As life's drama may somehow be,
performed on William Shakespeare's stage-
or of Langston Hughes's "The Big Sea."
Then recalling the sea's rescind,
it bows to her in the end.

Linda Hughes-Dorame

On Greeting Ralph Ellison

Ralph Ellison, a son of Oklahoma City
became a key writer of his century.
And on a clear, summer, day
admid stirring jubilation
warmly did he greet me at his library dedication.

As author of novels, short stories
and essays,
and like writers, Hurston, Hughes,
Wright and McCay-
he with thought, pen, word and measure
enriched our lives with immeasurable treasure.

Linda Hughes-Dorame

Mary McLeoud Bethune

It was a small blue book
holding words depicting the life
of Mary Mcleoud Bethune,
that was more than her biography
but an inspirational gift to me.
This great leader born in 1875
just two years prior to
reconstruction era's end
would uplift a flaming torch
from the ruins of despair
and bring forth wisdom, love, and care.
"Not for myself, but for others,"
was the maxim of her philosophy
and that there should and cannot be
discrimination and dual democracy.
We stand before these thresholds
confronting new frontiers
and we must bravely cross them as pioneers.

Linda Hughes-Dorame

Ode to My Dad

The gaiety of his laughter,
the warmth and wisdom of advice,
now is only memory
and echo in my life.
The adventures of his youth,
the war stories he'd tell,
and admired as black Indian
by baseball legend, Babe Ruth
I will remember well.
I'll remember not a character famed,
yet when taken to God in final rest,
his faith and brillance was proclaimed
by all those who'd known him best.
I'll remember accomplishments he made,
those awards he had achieved,
and his wish for fortune to bring,
the chance to march with Dr. King.
Alas, in tribute to my dad,
and for that remember most,
the tender for us he had
deserves a lasting toast.

Linda Hughes-Dorame

La Prunelle d'l'Oeil

To my husband Robert

If apples are the fruit of life,
perhaps they hole the love of life,
for my husband and I were,
heartily drinking apple cider,
while in Korea one day in June
as we met on a warm mid afternoon.
Twenty years now have past
and our love now will forever last.
La prunelle d'l'oeil! en francais,
for in Paris one bright Christmas day,
we again in celebration were
happily drinking apple cider.
Now on Christmas and New Year's day,
et pour notre anniversarie,
c'est dans le mois de mai-
we drink with our son and daughter
bubbling, sparkling, apple cider.

Linda Hughes-Dorame

In Memory of Mom

In memory of my mother, Anna Proctor

She's within our hearts forever.
Yet I know from afar,
She graciously moves above the stars.
And dad having waited long for her to come,
greeted her at the dawn of the new millennium.
The happiness they now share
does so overwhelm,
I can feel its glow from earth's realm.

Linda Hughes-Dorame

James Langston Hughes

To My Son and Daughter

Born in Joplin, Missouri in 1902
was a child named James Langston Hughes
destined to become a writer that
would become cultural emissary
and Harlem's Poet Laureate

Could his grandmother have known
that in their simple world forelorn,
nestled in historic Lawrence, Kansas
she'd provided knowledge and wisdom that
would nurture his literary genius-
and aspire him to greatness?

Perhaps from a heavenly realm
she later saw her beloved grandchild,
helping awaken the eye of justice
while of modern 20th century writers,
was among most original and versatile.

Linda Hughes-Dorame

God's Everlasting Flowers

To my sister Francis and cousin Angie

Our heavenly Father,
with loving care
nurtures me in despair,
and leads me along life's pathway
helping to meet the challenges of each day.
All my needs he does fulfill
as thee I serve and do thy will
And to witness the power of thee,
in bringing comfort to me
in the midst of my dull, dark, hours
is to receive thy awed, everlasting, flowers.

Linda Hughes-Dorame

Grandmother

In memory of my grandmother, Mariah Harris Proctor,
(1871-1965)

In the silent stillness of her room,
I can see my grandmother,
with pride and in solemn thought
sitting in her rocking chair,
her shoulders covered with knitted shawl
under African Indian braided hair.
Soft words of love and wisdom from her
answer to the warm call of "mother".
Her feeble hands resting in her lap
lifts my brother, David's hair to tap.
With brilliance he looks into her eyes,
and she into his while,
hers gleam with and Irish smile.

Linda Hughes-Dorame

A Tribute to Langston Hughes

In Commemoration of Mr. Hughes on his 100th birthday

On the 22nd of October you wrote
of a "mailbox from the dead."
But, "Life is for the living," you said.
"Death, is for the dead."
Thus so, and this is the day
I celebrate my birthday.
And on a November 27th,
you said, "I dream of a world,
where love will bless the earth."
I dream my little dark boy
will reach for your stars
for this is the day of his birth.
Alas, you met your "Dear Lovely Death,"
on a 22nd of May,
having planted your, "Tomorrow's Seed,"
with understanding, love, deed,
and ingenious use of word,
for those even yet to be born
as my daughter born on a 23rd.

Linda Hughes-Dorame

Autumn

Autumn enters with the spell
of decaying leaves and winds gently striking
nature's subdued serenity.
With a rushed whimpering breeze
that startles and shakes the trees,
it motions and gives the command
to rid themselves of their décor
and repeat their cycle once more.

Linda Hughes-Dorame

Aunt Mary

In Memory Mary Simpson Northington

Somewhere in the heavens
Aunt Mary tells her stories
and all the angels are charmed
happily with her smile
as once I was a child.
I remember her eagerly grasping
my hand on the cool spring days
as I watched passers-by in parade.
I remember the smell of her kitchen
with baked goodies and treats
that my siblings and I so loved to eat.

Linda Hughes-Dorame

A Salute to Joseph Simpson and the US Colored Troops

In Memory of the immortal United States Colored Troops and John Brown

There once lived a man on the Kansas plains
and Old Soldier was his honored name.
In 1870 he'd come from afar
after serving in the war.
And at the age of twenty-three,
he'd been a commissary sergeant
in the US Colored Infantry.
He'd fought to save the flag
and to end slavery,
at great risk as he was free.
Amid the wheat fields of Kansas
Joseph Simpson began
life as a farmer and businessman.
yet in the words of my mother,
her grandpa was a soldier,
and they called him Old Soldier.

Linda Hughes-Dorame

The Whale

At the bottom of the ocean deep,
are creatures we may never meet.
Some are large and some are small.
Whales are the largest of them all.
Whales shoot water from their snout.
They hold lots of fish in their mouth.
Some whales can jump so high,
it seems they are going to fly.
If I were a whale,
I'd jump high in the air
and in my own language would speak,
to everyone I would meet.

Maria Hughes-Dorame

A Blessed Christmas

Looking out at the starry night,
listening to harmony of carolers
outside my window,
I see smiles of joy and happiness
brightening everyone's face,
while watching the ocean of Christmas lights.
But looking at the nativity my soul and lifts,
knowing that the birth of Christ
is the greatest gift.

Maria Hughes-Dorame

The Lord

In Memory of my grandmother

Pray to the Lord with love and joy.
Pray to the Lord in day or night.
Pray to thee in heaven above
and pray to thee with heart-felt love.
When I feel the gentle wind
and when I pass the flashing sea,
I think of the Lord and how he made me.
We don't need to see the Lord
to know that he is there.
We know that he is everywhere.
The Lord is my comfort
and is my great friend,
who'll always be with me until the end.

Maria Hughes-Dorame

Silence

Silence can trap you.
It can put you in
another dimension
of total tranquility.
Silence can cover you
like a blanket protecting
you in its warmth.

Maria Hughes-Dorame

A Dreamer's World

Sometimes I imagine myself
above a mountaintop
looking out past the blanket
of green branches and the sun,
showering through the trees,
shining upon the vast terrain.
I hear the wind whispering
in the company of the clouds
and the singing of the birds
roaming the skies victoriously
and I can feel some silence
covering me like a blanket.
I can see for many miles
the rhythm of the dancing waterfalls
then I gulp my breath and the
whispers of the wind bring me
back to reality.

Maria Hughes-Dorame

A Dream Come True

To Grandma Rose

A dream come true,
does it taste like a fresh fruit?
Does it taste like chocolate
chip cookies fresh out of the oven?
A dream come true does it smell
like roses on a spring day?
Does it sound like the tide
slashing against the sand or the
chirping robin singing its song
among the clouds?
Does it sound like piano music
with the notes bouncing about
in the air?
Does it feel like a warm blanket
or a cozy fire on a cold day?
A dream come true is so beautiful.
So go after your dreams.
They will not die.

Maria Hughes-Dorame

Believe

Oh you should believe
In whatever you do.
The one who can make
the difference is you.
You should believe because if you do,
you can make your dreams come true.
If you follow your dreams and strive-
you will be surprised,
at what you can achieve,
if you believe.

Maria Hughes-Dorame

A Special Friendship

There's no mountain too high,
no river too low
that could tear us apart
because we will always be tight.
Insults and put-downs my rivals may say
but this friend is with me all the way.
I may get really nervous
and feel I want to hide,
but Jesus is always with me,
and will always be my guide.
I refuse to just give up,
or feel the feeling of defeat,
because with Jesus on my side,
I will not be beat.

Maria Hughes-Dorame

Giving

Giving is an act of love.
It can put a smile on a
person's face as warm
and nice as a big guilt.
Giving can mend a heart
that is broken and
wipe out sadness.
Giving can create
a blanket of happiness,
filling the void
in one's soul.

Maria Hughes-Dorame

Birds

I wonder what it would be like
to be a bird towering the skies
and listening to the whispers
of the wind, chirping the beautiful
song of freedom in the clouds
and watching from a distance
the sun flowering the world
with its warm light.
I wonder what it would be like
to fly so high in the company
of the glowing stars and full moon
almost as if it is smiling on
the sleepy earth or resting
upon a branch of blanket of green pine.

Maria Hughes-Dorame

God's Creation

Why are some too busy to rest their minds
on the beauty of God's creation?
Why are some too busy to hear God's almost
silent hyms of beauty?
Look at the creations and realize
the wonder of the magnificent glory.
Why do some ignore the sunset,
God's painting, or the graceful music
of the chirping of birds?
As I look about, I see trees,
their branches outstretched as though
worshipping God on high,
his magnificent power is revealed in nature
in his brilliant beauty.

Maria Hughes-Dorame

God Shine a Candle

God shine a candle when I go to bed.
God shine a candle when I rest my head.
God shine a candle during the night and
God shine a candle strong and bright.
God shine a candle when I fall asleep.
God shine a candle above the mountain peak.

God shine a candle through countries, cities, and states.
God shine a candle through ocean, rivers, and lakes.
And God when fast asleep, I pray your candlelight
to keep.

Maria Hughes-Dorame

My God I Thank You

My God I thank you
for hearing my prayers
for being my refuge
in times of despair.
You give me light
when things seem dark.
You mend and heal
the broken heart.
Whatever I do,
Whatever I say,
Whatever I think,
Whatever I pray,
will be for you
oh, God my strength
forever I will
praise your name.

Maria Hughes-Dorame

My Dream

My dream is a world where
everybody gets along,
where all people can
think of others
not only as humans
but as sisters and brothers.

My dream is a world
where people care about each other
and work together through thick and thin
where people can join hands together
as one family, working, learning,
and even having fun together.

I dream of a world where we never
hear of people dying from disease
there is no poverty and crime
and people aren't standing on
street curbs asking for money
and holding up signs-that is my dream.

Maria Hughes-Dorame

The Color Red

Red is an apple, crunchy, and sweet.
Red is a pop tart with raspberry filling.
Red is my school shirt worn every school day.
Red is the coat I wear outdoors to play.

Red are the beets I don't like at all.
Red is the big bouncing ball.
Red are the strawberries I love to eat.
Red is medium rare, cooked , meat.

Maria Hughes-Dorame

St. Mary

I can see a picture of Mary,
standing in glory,
a symbol of beauty and its song.
I can see a picture of Mary
with a golden crown, with diamonds
shining so brightly
as if there smiling.
I can see her surrounded
by a blanket of kindness and grace,
warm and comforting like a
beautiful blanket.

Maria Hughes-Dorame

The Rosary

For comforting prayers in times of pain,
full of love and joy for breaking hearts,
for prayers for those who are lonely,
how beautiful the rosary!
That great and worshipping poetry
reminder of our saviour's cross
and our mother Mary's crown of roses.
How beautiful the rosary for every
joyful eye. How beautiful the rosary
for every saddened sigh.
How beautiful the rosary for every
weeping soul and fallen tear,
reminder of our blessed Mother
to whom we bring our cries.
How beautiful is the rosary!

Maria Hughes-Dorame

The Monument Built for Me

I wish I could return to see
the monument that built for me.
It gives me a memory of the past,
a memory that will forever last.
My spirit stands on that place
where bravely I would fight
all the time, day and night
to win my freedom and my right.
And when the war was over,
and my fight was won,
the dangerous war was done,
the monument was built
and I will remember those like me
who fought and died to make us free.

Maria Hughes-Dorame

Waterfalls

Look at the waterfalls and realize
how it never ceases.
Realize the music it makes
almost like it's telling us
to stop and listen, to look at our gifts
and reflect and know the presence
of almighty God in our lives.
How this non-ceasing waterfall is
like God's love,
never stopping, and you know that-
God cares for you.

Maria Hughes-Dorame

The Mighty Eagle's Prayer

As I am in the sky and powerfully I fly.
I pray for pray for protection from hungry bears
who want to eat me.

I soar through the air.
I am a symbol of freedom in the mountain air.
I am the mighty eagle.

Maria Hughes-Dorame

Linda Hughes-Dorame

There is Music

In memory of my grandfather Memo, a great musician

There is music all around the world.
There is music in the shining of the moon.
There is music in your heart, find the tune.
Everywhere you go, there is music.
While you are riding down the road,
while you are walking down the street,
there is music in the people you meet.
There is music in a sun shiny day.
There is music in a rainy day.
It goes tap, tap, on my window pane.
There's music in the flowers that bloom.
There's music in the morning and noon.
There is music in trees swaying,
and gentle breezes.
There is music in the sparkling streams
and creeks.
There is music in the snowy
mountain peaks.
There is music all around the world.

Maria Hughes-Dorame

The Sunset

The beauty of the sunset
reflects upon my soul.
As I look toward the sky
in wonder I behold.
As my eyes view in awe
at the colors all around,
I see glistening in the waters
and listen to the sound
of the ocean's bouncing waves.

Maria Hughes-Dorame

The Rain

As I look out my window
I can see the rain.
It does a little dance
upon my window pane.
It can express my feelings
when I am feeling sad,
and when the sun comes out,
it's like again I'm feeling glad
and when I go to bed at night,
and I still hear the rain,
it plays a soft lullaby
until the very next day.

Maria Hughes-Dorame

The World War II Memorial

From 1941 to 1945
I wasn't even alive,
to see a war
spread far abroad.
The bombs were brusting
from land, sea, and air.
People were dying and starving
while others didn't care.
Men were leaving their families alone
while their wives were keeping home.

On a ship out to sea
or on the snow in Germany,
or in the air of blue, clouded skies,
one would wonder if he would live or die.
The war ended over 50 years ago plus,
but having the memorial is a must.
I only heard its stories from my
Dad you see,
as he fought to keep America free.

Frances A. Henderson

The School Bus Driver

As the school bus rolls down the street,
the children won't keep their seats,
and while the bus is in motion
one will surely get a notion
to throw paper of spit
on a schoolmate's shoes,
or call someone an ugly name
while playing with a pokemon
or Nintendo game.
Whatever the case may be,
we try smiling to all we see,
and when we stop at a bus stop or sign,
remember to be kind.
But maybe it can be rewarding,
as when kids one day finish school,
they'll kindly remember we bus drivers too.

Frances A. Henderson

For Each Other

For each other
our sister and brother,
crying and dying,
cold, hungry, and destitute.
It's a shame to see
it on TV.
People are suffering
because of man's
inhumanity to man.
Oh, how can they rest
on their fluffy, white, pillows
at night.
It should move you
just a little
to see that terrible sight.
It is good to show
how much you care.
Here today and gone tomorrow,
for wealth we gain
is only borrowed.
For each other,
our sister and brother

Frances A. Henderson

Linda Hughes-Dorame

Short Stories and a Play
by Maria Hughes-Dorame

The Temptation

Ten year old Carla was swinging near her friend, Jane. Everything was boring and no conversation was being said until Jane said, "I didn't tell you this, but I am going on vacation for 3 months. "Wow," said Carla, "I'm so happy for you." "I don't go on vacations until summer," Carla said.

Jane and Carla jumped off the swing to go to extended care, but before Jane could reach extended care, her dad came to pick her up from school. "Bye," said Jane, "I'm leaving tomorrow." "Don't be lonely," Carla said. "Have a fun trip."

Carla turned around to go to extended care, but before she was turning her back toward extended care, she saw Jane's diary on the ground. Jane had always been carrying her diary around school. "This must have dropped out of Jane's back pack while she was walking," Carla said to herself. "I could give it to the office, but Jane wouldn't like her diary in the principal's hands. Maybe it would be safer in my care," said Jane to herself. Carla put it in her backpack making sure no one saw her. She zipped up her backpack and then stopped to think. So while she was staying without Jane she was also staying with Jane's confidential thoughts. Then while picking up her backpack, her dad came.

While in the care with her brother and dad, she was quietly thinking if Jane knew she'd lost her diary. "You're awfully quiet today," her brother said. "Is anything wrong?" "No," said Carla. She knew if she told anyone, the diary would be taken to the principal's office.

When she got home, she laid on her bed and turned on the television. She took out Jane's diary and held it to her face. Carla sweated in the palm of her hand holding the diary and trying to watch the television. "Jane is probably looking for it," Carla said to herself. "Maybe I'd better give her a call and she if she is still at home." Carla ran downstairs and grabbed the telephone book and then ran back upstairs. Quickly she tried to find Jane's phone number. She found it and dialed it, hoping Jane would still be at home. Luckily, she was there. "Hello Jane, this is Carla. Remember when we jumped off the swing to go to extended care?" "Yes, I remember," said Jane. "And do you remember when your dad picked you up, and when we were walking?" You dropped your diary. You have to come and get it. My hands are sweating from temptation."

"OK, I understand," said Jane. "But I don't know the way to your house and we are leaving, how will I ever get there? Maybe you can mail it to me." "That will work," said Carla. Jane told her the address where she would be staying and Carla wrote it down on paper. "OK, I have it," said Carla. "I will explain everything to my parents." "Bye," said Carla. "Have a good vacation." Then they hung up the telephones and Carla went downstairs and explained everything to her parents. Her mom then began wrapping the diary for mailing to Jane. "Wait," said Carla. "I want to add a note." The note read,

"Don't worry, I did not read your diary."

That night Carla felt a whole lot better. Carla looked up at the stars and smiled because she knew Jane would soon have her diary to love and treasure.

A Friend

Boom! Rodney was flat on his face. The school bullies were running as fast as they could. I could tell the bullies were mean enough to push him. I felt like going over there and teaching those bullies some manners. But I didn't want to because I didn't want to get into trouble. With no hesitation, I went over realizing little marbles were all over the place. "Boy, those bullies should be kicked out of school immediately," I thought.

"Don't let those bullies get to you," I said. "Personally, I think they should be put in juvenile jail." But Rodney just laid there on his nose crying. Then he spoke, "I can't move my leg and it really hurts." "Oh, no!" I said. "It may be broken. Boy would I like to punch those bullies right in the nose. I'll help you."

"Thanks," he said smiling. We walked to the school's office with me supporting him and my arm over his shoulder. We reported what had happened as he sat on the office bench and I went back to pick up the marbles.

I put the marbles in my backpack. I thought about how to teach them a lesson, but then I decided the principal would take care of them and I'd pray for them when I got home. As I glanced at Rodney, he had a look in his eyes that said thanks. He had had no friends. Maybe I was his first friend.

The Nice Person's House of Doom

It was the day before Halloween. Sandy was at Alice's house. Sandy's parents said she had to be with Alice's parents if she wanted to go trick or treating. Sandy's older brother, Ron, was with she and Alice in Alice's room. They were discussing which home to go to first. Their parents said to just stay in the neighborhood so they didn't have to make a map. "This is going to be fun," said Sandy.

"Ya," but I don't think we should go to Miss Martin's," said Ron. "She is weird and lives all alone." "Well, I feel sorry for her and she is real nice," said Sandy. "You remember the time she saved that boy from a fire who lives at the end of the block?" said Alice. "If it weren't for her, we wouldn't see him again," said Alice. "I dare you to go to her house for

61

Halloween," said Ron. "So what? She's nice. That isn't to big of a challenge," said Sandy. "Ha, that's what they all say," said Ron. "Let's just ignore him eventhough he's older than us," said Alice. "He doesn't know any better. So they decided to go to Miss Martin's home first to show Ron a thing or two.

Later that night, they all left Alice's home to go trick or treating. Ron was dressed as a vampire. He had a black cape and play sharp teeth. Sandy was dressed as a witch. Alice also dressed as Cleopatra. They all walked to Miss Martin's house and then up her walk way and onto her porch and rang the door bell. "I think you are scared," said Sandy. "You are right. The only reason I am here is because you insisted on it," said Ron. Then all of a sudden, they heard Miss Martin coming to the door. She was singing happily as she came to the door. When she opened it, they saw a bright and cheerful lady. "Hello," she said. "I am so happy to see you." She gave them lots of candies and even invited them for a snack. They went in and talked to her for about 30 minutes. She was a kind and cheerful lady.

My Parents are Aliens from Outerspace

I sat on the living room floor flipping TV channels. Finally, something good was on the television. My parents were away and my big brother was watching me. Suddenly the door knob twisted and my parents came in the house. They sat on the couch. Then they sighed. Oh no, they always did that when they had to talk about something important. My brother and I just sat there in silence. "Kids, you probably won't believe this, but we your parents, are aliens from outerspace," said my dad. My brother and I just laughed. This had to be a joke. "Fine, get your jackets and follow us." My dad ordered.

I put on my plaid jacket and my brother put on his sports jacket. I still couldn't believe they were aliens from outerspace.

We followed my parents to the park. It was midnight so on one else was there. Wow! Then, we saw a hugh spacecraft in the park. Then my dad said, "hide behind the bushes." My brother and I stuned hid behind the bushes while our parents went toward the spacecraft.

A few minutes passed and we didn't see anything. We will never forget, then we saw something we will never forget. UFOs! UFOs! My parents pulled the skins off their faces and went into the spacecraft. They had purple faces with antenae on their heads. We thought we were dreaming and headed home in freight and climbed in bed.

The next morning my mom said after they had put their human skins back on, "Now do you believe us." My brother and I fell silent. We were in total shock. "Why did you guys come to earth? How did you become our parents and are we aliens too?" I asked. "No," my mom said. "You kids are not aliens. You were adopted." Then she said, "We lived on a planet in space called, Gonzopolis. we had heard about Earth and everyday we look down and wonder what it would be like to live there. So one day we went to our leader and asked if we could come here to visit. He said yes as he had been on Earth before, but we would need to have lung surgery. Without it we would have to wear breathing equipment all the time. So we had the lung surgery and boarded a space ship and came to earth. We landed in the same park where we were last night. We liked it here and decided to stay. At night we lived in the spacecraft with some alien friends, who decided to go back to Gonzopolis. In the daytime, we walked around town and learned about humans, how to speak the language, and then obtained jobs in town. Later we bought this home and wanted human children so we adopted you kids. We love you very much."

My brother and I were lost for words. We knew now it was true. I couldn't think of anything to say. I just ate my breakfast.

We never told anyone they were aliens from outerspace. We love them as if they were human parents.

Meeting a Friend

It was Friday of the first week of school. As usual Sandy sat on the school balancing beam, watching the other kids play with their friends. Despite of all her loneliness, she was excited for she was told she was going to get a surprise when she came home. And she thought about it, the frown on her face turned into a smile.

It was a puppy, a cute golden retriever. Little did she know how much she would get closer to her over the years. And she did. She got so close to her she would hear a sad howl in the distance every time she would leave for school.

"Good girl, Shamrock," said Sandy praising her for staying as she went to go have supper. After supper, since she didn't have school the next day, she watched

TV until she was too tired. While she was asleep she thought she heard a cat hiss, but she went back to sleep.

The next morning she looked and she was gone. "Shamrock is gone!" Said Sandy panicking. She yelled to the whole family could hear. She got dressed so fast she tripped a few times. She raced to the car. They rode around, but saw no glimpse of Shamrock. The whole day depended on looking for her but she was no where to be found.

It was the beginning of summer. Sandy and her two older brothers at home on the front porch, dripping wet because of a water ballon fight. Then all of a sudden she saw a new family. As Sandy got a closer look, her mouth fell open. It was no doubt, Shamrock.

The dog followed the girl as they wen to Sandy's house. After they introduced themselves, Sandy told her she thought it was Samrock. Emily, the girl, fell silent. "Here is your dog. I love her but she belongs to you," said Emily with a smile. "Thanks," said Sandy. Emily sighed. Then she smiled. Before she walked off she turned around as asked, "Would you like to come to my house?" Sandy said yes and she realized she had her two best friends.

A Lonely Friend

It was the most boring recess I ever had in my entire life. The breeze clapped against my face, biting my nose and cheeks. I buried my face in my coat, breathing in warm breaths. It was like sitting next to soothing fire after spending time in the biting snow. After warmth pressed against my face, I pushed my head out of my coat. From the corner of my eye, I saw a little girl hunched over the fence. I saw that her jacket was torn and dirty and messy hair hit her eyes. As she got it out of the way, I saw her hands were bitten from the bitter chill that shrivered and traveled through my body. I couldn't understand why she would walk all the way over here. A strange feeling came over me to go and talk to her and I did. I was nervous and wanted to walk away but I couldn't. It was like my feet were planted to the ground until we had a friendly conversation.

I just stood there and tried to say something, but words wouldn't come out of my mouth. Fortunately, I was saved from pressure when the girl said, "Hi." I said, "Hi, why aren't you in school?" I couldn't help asking her. Her face turned red and my heart started beating a mile a minute. Seeing she was uncomfortable with the question, I quickly changed the subject. "What is your name?" I asked. "Laura," she replied. Her eyes were wide staring at the kids who were having fun.

"Where do you live?" I asked. "475 Cox Street." She said. She shrivered from the bitter cold. I couldn't help but give her my school sweat shirt. She put it on and her shrivering stopped. Eventhough, I was cold the friendliness of her smile made me feel warm. I smiled back. "What is your name?" Laura asked. "Shawna," I replied. "Oh," said Laura.

Suddenly the bell rang. Somehow I had an inch of hope that I might see her again. After school I didn't forget the conversation I had with Laura. In fact, I couldn't get it off my mind. I knew something was strange about her but I couldn't put my fingers on it.

I thought the weekend was going to be normal, but I was wrong. That weekend, I learned the truth about Laura. It all started during breakfast. "So what if we go to the mall today?" My mom asked. "Sure I'd love to," I said. My father was away on a business trip and I was home with my mom and 17 year old brother. T. J. was a senior so we decided at the beginning of the year to be nice to each other as he would be going away to college. I asked T.J. to come with us and he said OK.

While we were at the mall, we passed by the clothing store. "May I go in the clothing store?" I asked my mom. "Sure, she said. The food stand is close by. I will go buy you some lunch. Don't go too far and T. J. stay close by and watch your sister." I hated it when she said that.

As I looked around the clothing store, I bumped into Laura. "Hi, Laura," I said with a bright smile. Where are your parents?" I watched as her face turned red. She took a big sigh and pulled me over to a corner.

"Shawna, I was going to tell you something that might freak you out, and I don't blame you if you tell," she said. I was waiting at school one day for my parents. It was very late. I was worried and surprised. I thought my parents would pick me up soon but they didn't. I haven't seen them since. When I got home I was tired and went to sleep. I cried and waited for hours, but they didn't come.

The flashback disappeared and all that was left was the thick silence in the air. When T. J. came over, Laura walked away. But I saw she was crying. "Mom has the lunch," T. J. said seeing the shocked look on my face. He asked, "Is something wrong?" I told him everything from that recess I met Laura.

After a week, I thought of a way to help Laura. Luckily, I saw her during my recess. I decided to talk to her about it. I was going to ask her if she could sleep over at my house. I asked her and she said yes.

After convincing my mom. Everything was set. The next time I met her would be a my sleepover. When I woke up the morning she was supposed to come, I had excitement I couldn't control. My family knew about Laura so now there were no secrets. "I hope Laura likes us," said T.J. finishing his toast. "I'm sure she will," I said eating my eggs.

....

We picked up Laura at her home. She had an excited look on her face. I was happy when I saw her wearing my sweatshirt. Then mom drove up to the pizza place and we had hot cheese pizza before going home.

When we got home, I got an idea. Since she was alone, could she live with us and share my room? She liked the idea and I said I was going to ask my mom. "Of, course she can," said my mom. "As a matter of fact your dad and I have already received permission from the authorities or her to stay with us for a while." "Oh thank you, thank you," she said hugging my mom and me. I turned around and my mom had a smile on her face. Laura said, "Now I have a new family and I will be happy with them."

Marianna Finds Faith

Dedicated to my Mom and Dad and the Families of the Victims of September 11th

Unfortunately it was not a normal day in Marianna's village of Wolluf. The sun was shining and its reflection made the waters in that part of Senegal, Africa look like pearls. Still it was not a normal day.

Marrianna was one of those sad little girls who had seen a new emergency in the village. And this time the victim, was her own brother. Marianna's mother, Benada, had been taking her break at the village hospital. Then Marianna ran in frantically crying.

"What happened?" Asked Benada.

"It's Malik! He was horsing around with the boys in the village. Then he fell and hit his head on some sharp rock. He's very wounded mother!"

"That's terrible!" Shouted Benada. "Well, God is with Malik. We should have hope." "Hope," shouted Marianna. "There is no hope. It's all over. He won't heal. He'll die soon. Only bad will come out of this!" Marianna was now hysterical and those cries were so loud, they could be heard throughout the hospital.

Before she could respond, Malik was carried into the hospital by some strong men, who had sweat pouring down their concerned faces. Malik was clearly unconscious and had blood pouring from his head. Benada took a deep breath, and said a prayer. She was now ready to work with that faith that shaped her heart. But Marianna couldn't watch. She ran outside and under the shade of a tall tree.

There she waited frantically. "He'll die! He'll die! It's obvious, he'll die! Mamma's wrong! There is no hope. It's over." She thought. There she sat in her special spot. She knew that her father, who had died during a terrible drought had prayed here, for his family's protection. Marianna had had never met her father, but somehow, in this spot she felt close to him. These thoughts of her father relaxed her, and she fell asleep. She was obviously exhausted and was asleep for hours.

"Marianna, Marianna," whispered the sweet voice of her mother. Marrianna woke to see the beautiful colors of the sunset, yellow, orange, and blue that swam across the sky. Benada gently grabbed her by the hand, and led her into the hospital. Here she was surprised to find that Malik lay on a mattress alive and awake.

"Malik my brother how are?" Shouted Marianna. "I'm OK Marianna come over here." Marianna moved to the side of the mattress. "Mother told me you were expecting that I'd die, but I'm still here and much better. Papa used to tell me to always carry with you, a little bit of faith and to trust in God. Take it from me. Don't think so badly all the time." Oh, Malik, that's a lesson I'll always remember. "But you see Marianna, even if Malik had not recovered, God would have helped us in other ways," said her mother.

Marianna now understood and she smiled vowing to never speak negatively again.

The Red Candles

Imagine a setting at church. The stained glass windows bring in a mixture of orange, purple, brown, blue, and red to the surroundings. It's after mass. Now my mom and my brother watch as red candles melt and are blazing as part of the room's tranquility. The servers are clearing the altar. We go light a red candle and we feel the chilling wind, for the the open door lets in the dance of the brisk morning air. We light a red candle during this time in the Christmas season in remembrance of Grandma who is now with God in heaven and died during the Christmas season.

We started the tradition this last year after Grandma died. The idea came to my mom in a dream. She dreamed of Grandma appearing to her and handing her red candles. Mom says that the dream is the comforting sign to enjoy our Christmas and not be sad because Grandma's gone.

A few days later, we lighted a red candle at home to remind us of Grandma in mom's dream. I watched the flame with my mom sitting across from me on the blue and pink couch with flowers intermixed. As I watched the illuminating flame walked me back to those loving memories of Grandma with her sweet voice that would talk to me, her smile that would warm anyone's heart.

Christmas morning we feel the warmth of holiday joy and the lighted candle brings Grandma's presence lingering in the magic of the holiday. And that's what really makes it Christmas.

A New Life

A sad, lonely, face looked up at me. My student took a big sigh, picked up her backpack and left. At that moment, I wished I had something that would have made her feel better. I, as a teacher never liked to see a student sad and lonely. My heart felt heavy with sorrow. I pushed back my bangs, picked up lesson books and papers and left, letting the left-over sorrow in that room follow me all the way home.

After I had finished correcting my papers, I watched TV just like I always did when a problem lay ahead. I took a big sigh. My student didn't fit-in. She had just moved from a small cottage in the prairie to a big city in New York. It was strangely similar to my childhood. I lay back and left my mind to drift to the past of when I was a little girl.

I grew up in a small town in the Ozark Hills. Being away from city life was fine with me. I loved going fishing with my father and my older brothers. Sometimes, I would dream about living in the big city, but I would wake up and once again love where I lived and I thought that would never change, but I was wrong.

One day father let us go fishing by ourselves. I was surprised. Why would father do that? I figured my parents must have wanted to talk about something.

"Sure they do," said my oldest brother, Thomas. "It must be important," said Elliot, my second oldest brother. "Come quickly!" Yelled Thomas holding up a big fish on his line. We cheered with joy. I was so happy about the fish. I completely forgot what was going on with my parents. "Let's go home and show father, and mother will be cooking a big fish for dinner tonight," said Thomas. "Yes," I said.

"Father, father!" We all yelled, the fish dangling on the line, "We caught a big one today father," said Elliott. "All by ourselves," I said. But when I saw a strange look on father's face, I knew something was wrong. My brothers knew it too. "What is it father?" I asked. "I'll tell them," said mom. She took a big sigh. "Kids we're moving to the big city of New York because we think it is best for you to go to a larger school to get an education. "I couldn't believe it. This was where I grew up, and now I would be moved into a different environment. The big city. How were we ever going to manage?

As the days of packing up and getting ready carried on, I tried my best to change their mind but it was no use. In a few days, we would be ready to go leaving the home we treasured forever.

After weeks of getting ready, we were all packed up ready to go. Seeing the land from far away as we left was beautiful. With tears in my eyes, I said good-bye to homeland. I watched as the Ozark Hills disappeared in the distance.

Chapter Two

When we finally arrived in New York, everyone watched as we drove close to the Statute of Liberty. Then we stopped to honor it. Later after we'd arrived at our new apartment, it looked so different from our small cottage back home. It was a whole lot bigger than I had expected. It took a few days to get unpacked and register for the Catholic school, I'd attend, for my parents to begin work, and get situated. But we did it.

This morning was special. It was our first day of school. I hated waking up early and putting on a uniform, but other than that I was excited. When I saw the school, I was nervous and surprised. I could hear kids everywhere. When my parents had left, I could hear my heart beating.

Everyone was silent when I walked into the extended care room, but came over to introduce themselves. I thought they would be friendly to me, but when, I asked what dominoes were, they laughed and teased. That hurt my feelings. I just sat alone in a corner trying not to cry. I saw a young girl with a paper come into the room. Her blond hair hid her face. She looked over at me. Her eyes were filled with guilt. She came over. "Hi," she said with a smile. I smiled back. I thought she was pretty nice. A girl walked over to her. "What are you doing talking to the girl who doesn't even know what dominoes are?" That's not nice!" She said. "Besides I can talk to whoever I want." She said madly. Then the girl mumbled something and walked away. The blond haired girl smiled at me, "I'm Shannon," she said. "I'm Laura," I said. We shook hands. "So what are dominoes anyway?" I asked.

"Come on and I will show you." I followed her. She pulled out a black box. Inside were little squares with dots on them. Really, it was pretty fun when we played.

Just before we were about to put the dominoes back, a bell rang. It startled me a little. "Don't worry," she said. "It tells you, you got to go to class." "Oh," I said embarrassed. "First we to the gym and then to class," she said. "OK," I said.

When we were in the gym she asked. "No offense, but why didn't you know what dominoes were?" "Well," I began, "I lived in a small town in the Ozark Hills. I wasn't around many people, so I didn't know what dominoes were and what other games are."

"Oh," she said, "I will teach you some other games after school if you'd like." "Thank you." I said. Then strangely she put her hand up. I didn't know what she was doing so I asked. "What are you doing?" "It's what friends do," she said. When I heard the word friends, I smiled. She said it was a "high five." I gave up a "high five." I really did have a friend. I glanced over, so did Thomas and Elliott. I smiled.

When I saw the classroom, it was so big. The teacher stood at the front of the room. Behind her was a green board. "Oh, Laura," said the teacher, "here's your desk." She pointed to a desk at the front of the room. I was happy my desk was next to Shannon's.

"She doesn't know anything. I don't see why you want to talk to her," said a girl sitting next to us. I hated it when people made fun of me. When I was about to say something, Shannon spoke up. "Michelle, why don't you just lay off?" Then everything quieted down.

"Class today, I introduce our new student, Laura Ramen," the teacher, Miss Janice, said. "Please stand up, Laura." I stood up and then sat down again after she explained the class rules.

As the days went by almost everything seemed different. During language, Miss Janice had an announcement to make. "Class I will assign you to write a 2-page essay on something you thought would be hard, but turned out to be easy." It was like the teacher had read my mind. I knew exactly what to write about. Shannon and I were becoming best friends. I could tell it in my bones. Then the bell rang for recess.

We headed for the school playground. During recess, I thought a lot about the essay. Since Shannon was my friend, it sure made everything a lot easier.

Eventhough a lot of other kids thought I wasn't smart at all.

Michelle came up to us after school and was making fun or something for Shannon and I being friends. It made Shannon so angry she almost cried. I couldn't take it anymore. "Leave her alone!" I said sternly with my arms crossed. "Go away and quit making fun of my friend and me or I will tell Miss Janice." Michelle sighed, "I'm sorry," she said. "I won't make fun of you anymore." We both smiled. "Why don't you play with us?" I said. "Really," said Michelle. "Ya," said Shannon. "We can lot of fun, the 3 of us."

Two days later, when I decided to start my essay, I had no trouble. I wrote about how hard it was to move to the big city away from my last environment and how Shannon had helped me make my experience

93

good. But, I said that the class has also helped me to go through the change and it was true. When they stopped judging me, they came to like me and help me a lot.

On My Own

My older brother, Austin is 1 years old and I, Sally am 11 years old. We sat at the table eating dinner an couldn't help thinking that our parents had been acting weird all day. The table was full of silence. Somebody had to break the ice, and that somebody was going to be me. "Mom, dad you have been acting weird all day. What is going on?"

I asked in curiousity. Mom said, "Well, Sally your father and I are leaving on Saturday for five days. My brother and I did not say a word. We finished our dinner without saying a word. After dinner I headed for my room. For some reason it made me feel sad to even think of having my parents away for days. Days passed and finally the day came when they heard my parents mention having anyone to help mind the house.

At breakfast, the table was full of silence just like the day when Austin and I had first heard the news of their leaving. I felt like I was a grownup full of responsibilities. There wasn't a lot of eating or drinking, just thinking.

After breakfast, we went into the living room to wait for their ride. Mom gave up a list of instructions and said they would telephone us everyday and left the address and telephone number showing how to contact them. As soon as the ride pulled up to our driveway, there were a lot of hugging and saying, "we'll miss you." As my parents headed out the front door and into the car we started waving continuously until the car disappeared into the distance.

We waited on the couch looking at our street wondering if our parents would come back saying, they didn't want to leave us for 5 days. Unfortunately, that didn't happen. So we all got up and watched television until we became hungry and wanted to eat lunch.

"Do you think we can live on our own," I asked as we investigated the refrigerator. Truefully, no." said Austin. "We don't know how to cook or drive. I don't know what I am going to do." He sounded like my dad worrying about bills, insurance payments, and bounced checks. There was tuna casserole in the refrigerator and we heated it in the microwave oven. Suddenly, an idea came to me just like a flash of lightning. We could hire a housekeeper to cook for us, and keep the house in order while we were at school. Oh yes, and drive us to school and places we needed or wanted to go.

Austin said, "You know for once Sis, I agree with you." A smile brightened on his face.

After lunch we went into the dining room and flipped through the phone book to find a housekeeper. We found one with an agency and dialed the number. Austin spoke when the phone was answered.

"Hello, is this the housekeeper agency," asked Austin in his most grownup voice. "OK we can wait to have a housekeeper," said Austin with disappointment. Almost all of my life I wanted to be an adult. Now I knew how many responsibilities were before them. The main question was am I growing up too fast?

The next day a housekeeper came to our house for an interview. I was relieved when Austin hired her. When she arrived the next morning, she told me, "My name is Miss Williams." I asked her how many days did she plan to be here trying to sound as polite as ever. "Seven days a week," she said. Was this too much? Austin pulled me aside for a discussion. I explained to him that this was way too much, but then I thought, a full-time housekeeper would be a lot of help.

Finally, no more marking on the calendar. Today my parents were coming home. I was very happy and relieved. Austin was too, except he didn't ask them about hiring a housekeeper. My parents had told him that he should take a homemaking class offered at his high school, but of course, he didn't take it. Now he knows what my parents mean when they say, that knowing how to cook will help him a lot one of these days. He told me his best friend was taking a cooking class and knows how to cook.

We finished our breakfast of sausage, eggs, and toast. Then suddenly, the door bell rang. We ran to the window to see who it was. We saw our parents standing on the porch just waiting to hug us when we opened the door. We ran to the door with a smile almost as bright as the sun. We opened the door and hugged them. It was the happiest day of my entire life.

The next day...

"Ouch," I said. I fell and scraped my knee on the cement. My shoes weren't tied.

I tied them, and went to ask the recess teacher if I could get an icepack. She said yes. I walked to the door of the teacher's lounge and was about to knock. When suddenly I heard someone with a voice like our housekeeper's. It was her voice. She was applying for a job there. When we had told her we didn't need her anymore, we didn't know she didn't have a job.

The Next Day

I came home and stood on the porch. Dad didn't say anything. I think he wanted me to see for myself. In the house, Miss Williams was sitting at the kitchen table. She looked tired. I had five dollars in my piggy bank and Austin had ten. Miss Williams was now our permanent housekeeper. Maybe if my parents added some money, we could order a pizza to celebrate. Now I felt like she was part of our family. We all ate pizza that night.

So finally, Austin did take the homemaking class. He told me he will take a class in homemaking until he graduates. Soon he will also have a car.

Friends for Life

Characters:

Mary
Amy
Mary's Mother and Father
Amy's Mother and Father
Annie
Annie's Mother and Father
Annie's brother and Sister
Narrator

Mary is a slave girl who has a desire to read and write. One day she meets a girl named Amy, who is willing to teach her and be her friend.

Act 1, Scene 1

The scene is in front of the home of Mary Williams of Lawrence, Kansas in the early 1930s. The Simpson family has just arrived in horse and buggy for a visit to their 100 year old Aunt Mary's home. Mary's son is working in the garden. Mary comes out to greet them.

Annie: Hi Aunt Mary
Mary: Hello Annie and all of you. Come in and sit down.
Annie: I want to hear about the time when your friend taught you to read and write and how she taught you the alphabet.
Mary: Sure I will tell you.

The whole family is sitting down eager to listen. The story begins.

Act II: Scene 1

Mary and her parents are working in the field on a plantation in Missouri.
Mary: Mama, I want to learn how to read and write.
Narrator: Mama's face is stern.
Mama: Don't be foolish!
Narrator: Then papa adds with a stern face.
Papa: Your mother does not want you to learn.
Narrator: Mary whispers to herself secretly.
Mary: I still wish I could escape.

Narrator: But Mama hears.

Mama: What makes you think you could escape from....She pauses.

Mama: Just continue your work child.

Narrator: Meanwhile the slave owner's daughter, Amy, is looking around to see if slaves are working. She is very sad as she walks around. She then stops at Mary. Mary is scared.

Mary: I'se working Miss, I'se working.

Amy: Don't worry. I won't hurt you.

Mary: Oh thank you, Miss.

Amy: My name is Amy.

Mary: You really nice.

Amy: Thank you. Do you want to learn how to read and write?

Narrator: Mary is afraid to answer, but in almost a whisper says.

Mary: Yes, Miss Amy.

Amy: I will be willing to help you.

Mary: Thank you, Miss. When we get a chance?

Amy: Look like I have a chance now. We have to go where no one can see us.

Narrator: They go to a place where no one can see them.

Amy: Let's start with the alphabet.

Mary: They call it ABCs.

Amy: Right.

Mary: So what's the first letter?

Amy: A like the first letter in my name. It can be also sounded out as ay like the words can and has.

Mary: What is the whole alphabet?

Narrator: Amy says and writes the whole alphabet.

Mary: That really long.

Amy: There are what are called 26 letters.

Narrator: She erases the letters.

Amy: I think I have to be home before my parents find out I am gone.

Mary: Yes. Miss Amy. I have to go back to work too.

Amy: Bye.

Mary: Bye Miss Amy.

Amy: I'm coming back to teach you more.

Narrator: Amy returned to teach Mary again and again. She would teach her while everyone else was asleep. They became the best of friends.

ACT III. Scene1: At Mary's home in the slave quarters.

Mary's papa: Darling, I know something weird is going on.

Mary's mama: I think your are right and I think it has to do with Amy.

Mary's papa: We got to talk to Mary.

Narrator: It is late at night and Mary has just finished her lessons with Amy. She luckily makes it to her quarters before her parents see her come in the door.

Mama: We know something is going on and it has to do with you.

Mary: You are right mama and papa. It has to do with my wish. They have a long talk.

Her parents are excited and scared. They tell her she must stop trying to learn.

ACT IV. Scene1: Amy's house. She has just sneaked back in her bed through the window.

Amy's father: Where have you been?

Amy's mother: Have you been teaching Mary? What are you teaching her?

Amy: Yes, papa I have taught her the ABCs.

Amy's papa: Well, you are teaching the wrong person, a slave!

Amy's mother: He is right. You are never to go around her again. Do you understand me!

Narrator: Inspite of the risk they both took. Mary and Amy continued to be friends and found ways to come together and Amy taught Mary to read the Bible.

Mary: I finally learned to read and write. Thank you Amy. You are a friend for life.

Amy: Now I will help you escape.

Narrator: One day Mary escaped from slavery.

This play is based on a story that was told to my grandmother by her great

Aunt who was nearly 100 years old in the 1930s.

The Life and Times of Joseph Simpson
by Linda Hughes-Dorame

I often heard my mother and my Aunt Mary speak of my great grandfather, Joseph Simpson, who they called, "Grandpa Simpson." They spoke of him with great pride in the accomplishments be as a black union soldier and 1870 Kansas settler had made. My curiosity of this ancestor caused me to begin research to gather information about him and to gain information about conditions which impacted the lives of early Kansas's black population.

Joseph Simpson was born June 1, 1841 to free parents, Patrick and Melissa Simpson in Warrensburg, Missoui. He was their eldest son and one of eight children. Their other children were: Arminda,

Armanda, Millie, Harriet, Mary, Washington, and Lewis.

Virtually nothing is known of his early life, but by the year 1862, he had become a farmer in Warrensburg and apparently had learned to read and write. Also in 1862, on April 14th, he married my great grandmother, Marinda Hughes. She was originally from Kentucky and is believed to have been a slave there. Her first marriage had ended in 1860 with the sale of her husband, Richard Collins, who later died before the Civil War. It is said that she was related to the paternal family of the writer Langston Hughes, whose ancestors were also from Kentucky. The Simpsons would have eight children: Mandy who was died within 2 years of her birth in 1864, Joseph Wesley born April 3, 1864, John born November 3, 1867, James born July 27, 1870, Anna born November 3, 1871, Edgar born

November 8, 1872, William who was born and died in 1874, and Nelson who was born on March 22, 1875.

At the age of 22, shortly after their marriage, my great grandfather enlisted in the Union army for 3 years. The newly wedded Mrs. Simpson, went to live with her sister-in-law, Mary during this turbulent time. He was mustered into Company F of the 65th United States Colored Infantry at Benton Barracks on February 24, 1864 by Colonel Bonneville.

Enlistment in the Union army was perceived by black soldiers as both an opportunity to strike back at slavery and to prove their worth and loyalty to the country.

However here as elsewhere, they felt the biting stings of prejudice. Colonel Higginson, in his memoirs writes that, "They were under constant surveillance. A single mutiny- a single miniature Bull Run, a stampede of desertions and it would have been all over with us; the party of distrust would have got the upper-hand, and there might not have been during the whole contest, another effort to arm the Negro."

The First South Carolina Volunteers was the first slave regiment mustered into the army. They were under the command of Major-General Butler of New Orleans. The "First Kansas Colored Troops," was recruited earlier, but had not been mustered in the army. The Second South Carolina and the 54th Massachuetts followed in early 1863.

Their periods of enlistment were usually longer than whites. They were seldom promoted and were given old weapons. Their pay was lower than that of whites. When black soldiers were wounded, they were carried from the battlefield with an afterthought.

Upon arrival in hospitals, they received poor care. If captured by the Confederates, they were either immediately executed or treated as runaway slaves rather than as prisoners of war. Yet inspite of these difficulties, most black soldiers served with honor.

The Navy had been opened to free blacks before the Emancipation Proclamation.

In 1861 the navy enlisted former slaves due to a shortage of manpower. By end of the war, there were approximately 29,000 black sailors making up a quarter of the Union fleet. four black sailors received the Naval Medal of Honor.

The contention that blacks would make poor soldiers was proven to be absolutely absurd. Colonel Higginson wrote, "That it was quite the contrary. They took to rapidly to drill and did not object to discipline. They were fully aware of their mission and the importance of the contest. They were neither jealous or suspicious towards their officers or showed no resentment towards the government. They were willing to risk their lives, even if paid nothing."

In the evenings camp lights glimmered in the tents and many used this time to learn to read and write. The love for the spelling book was inexhaustible for many. Usually too sounds of glee and laughter and a drummer's throb could be heard from far away in the tents. Wild killdeer would plover, flit and wail with a haunting sense while sounds from half prayer meetings were heard. These prayer meetings had shouting around fires made of palm-leaves. Some men sang quaint Negro Methodist chants with a regular drumming of their feet and clapping of their hands. Then there was a sort of snap sound and the spell would break with silence and then sighing and laughter.

The regiment in which my great grandfather served, the 65th Infantry Regiment would face combat with the Battle of Port Hudson. This battle began on May 23, 1863.

It is significant due to its duration of 48 days and the use of regular US black army troops for combat for the first time in the war.

Port Hudson was a Confederate stronghold on the Mississippi. It was strategically important to the South to protect Vicksburg, Mississippi from the Union naval fleet.

When Vicksburg fell to Union forces on May 22, 1863, federal forces seized the fort.

The Confederates had also been defeated on August 5, 1862 at the Battle of Baton Rouge.

The black soldiers fought heroically, making desperate charges on the Confederate batteries. They suffered heavy losses but continued to maintain their positions as they advanced. After the seize, the garrison at Port Hudson became a recruiting center for African American troops until the summer of 1866.

My great grandfather was appointed Corporal on March 12, 1865. On April 14th, he was promoted to Sergeant but reduced to Corporal on August 11, 1865. Surprisingly to me after this turn of promotion, he was again promoted to regimental commissary sergeant on September 18, 1866. He held this position until he mustered out on January 8, 1867 in Baton Rouge and returned to his home in Warrensburg, Missouri.

In 1870, Joseph Simpson and his family, including his parents and brothers and sisters settled in Bloomington, Kansas, a small community on the outskirt of Lawrence, Kansas. By now, the community had come to be regarded as largely a black community.

It was distinguished as having been one of the nine little sister communities located on the Wakarusa Basin, the Valleys of Rock Creek, Deer Creek, Washington Creek, and the Wakaursa River. These communites were the site of what came to be known as "Bleeding Kansas." They were host to John Brown and proudly provided him a warm reception.

In Bloomington, my great grandfather purchased an old-style plantation house with steep stairways and 13 rooms along with 50 acres from Elizabeth Berkau, one of the town's original founders. Evidence later showed that the house was probably once a station on the underground railroad. He paid $1000.00 for the home in which he moved his family and converted the front of it to a store in which he sold goods to neighbors.

He prospered as a farmer and businessman eventually purchasing more land and moving his business to a separate building on the premises. My mother spoke of the rock house that was used as a refuge from tornadoes.

The black residents of Bloomington and the neighboring town of Clinton were most commonly farmers who found enjoyment with several major events during the year.

There was little interest among them in Independence Day on July 4th, but Emancipation Day was fully celebrated on August 1st. There was an all day picnic, speeches and a ball game. George Washington, brother-in-law of Joseph Simpson, was active organizer and participant in this event. He addressed the crowd with accounts of his Civil War episodes and how he and his fellow black soldiers had fought so heroically. On June 26, 1894, an article was featured in the Lawrence Journal describing this celebration. It cited it as being held in George Washington's grove. Among those present was the former auditon, of the State and several other nothworthies. In the previous year, as many as 1000 people had attended the event at the grove.

Every fall, money raising activities were held. These usually featured pie suppers, box socials, cake walks, or a raffle with the winner receiving a blanket or a turkey roaster. These events were usually held at the local school or church.

Christmas was celebrated with annual school programs. The children presented wrapped gifts they had crafted to their parents.

Two turns of events in Kansas in 1874, were the Temperance Movement and the grasshopper invasion. The Temperance movement, highly political, would secure Kansas as a dry state for fifty years.

Grasshoppers growing in size and number invaded farmlands and in some areas, entire fields were carpeted. Thankfully, on June 12th, they suddenly rose in the air and few away to the great relief of the distressed residents.

Floods were commonplace in the Bloomington-Clinton Communities. There was peroidic flooding of the Rock Creek and the Wakarusa Rivers. The Rock Creek Flood of 1895 was particularly destructive. The residents also had to contend with elecrical storms and tornadoes some which were devastating.

Inspite of these difficulties, black farmers played a significant role in Eastern Kansas. The media has mostly ignored or obscurred the realities of the lives of these settlers in the west and on the prairies.

The number os blacks in Kansas rose from 17,108 in 1870 to 43,107 in 1880. They were spurred to emigrate to kansas because it had come to be known as the "garden of the west." Kansas had good, abundant land and was more easily acquired than land in the south. Freed men in the south usually lacked the resources to purchase land and southern whites were unwilling to advance them credit or sell land to them. As a result, black emigration agents, such as george marlouce of louisiana reported to blacks the abundance of land and opportunities in kansas.

In 1881, black farmers had established 12 agricultural colonies in Kansas. Nicodemis, having been one of them, was founded in 1877. Most of these colonies were soon disbanded. However, some remained viable well into the early 1900s. By 1900 African Americans owned 3,721 Kansas farms with an estimated value of $3.7 million. This number continued to increase and in 1910, the value of their lands had become almost $8.5 million.

Junerius Groves was one of the most properous of black farmers. In 1907, he was reported to have been the world's largest grower of Irish potatoes. At the age of 48, he owned more than 40 square miles of land in several Kansas counties.

These successes led leaders in the community to highly advocate the ownership of land, but unfortunately, black land ownership was also on the decline in the early 1900s. One reason for this was the lack of the ability to compete with the more sophisticated farming methods among poor black farmers, lacking resources to acquire the machinery needed. More and more black Kansans moved to the cities seeking employment and opportunities.

Joseph and Marinda Simpson lived modesty during the early 1900s in their 13 room farmhouse. Dramatically saddening to them was the death of their only surving daughter, Anna, in 1892. She subcommed to pnenomia as it is said she had the habit of usually walking barefoot. My mother was named in honor of her by her older brother, Joseph Wesley.

Melissa Simpson died in 1901 at the age of 87. Her husband, Patrick Simpson died in 1904 as the ripe old age of 104. They were remembered especially in the community for donating land that housed the building for the first African Methodist Episcopal church in Rock creek valley.

Joseph Simpson died on June 17, 1921 with conjestive heart failure. His wife, Marinda died in

1927. Their property and business was passed to their son and my grandfather, Joseph Wesley. My mother , Anna, was born on this property in 1923. She died in 1999.

The depession of the 1930s, deeply felt, caused my grandfather to sell his property at a sheriffs sale to Mrs. Demeritt for $4214.80 on december 13, 1927.

Now this property and the entire community no longer exists and is burried under the waters of clinton lake. However the legacy of the those who lived

And worked in these communites will live forever and the heroic efforts of the black settlers who lived here will tower above any walls of prejudice.

Marinda Hughes Simpson

Nelson Simpson, Jimmie Simpson, Joseph Simpson

(3 sons of Joseph and Marinda Simpson)

Loffrence Skansas
Jan The 26 19.14
Nelson Simpson Dear Son
I thought I would write you
a few lines to let you Know
that only tabale well I have the
reumitsome in my armes & i
my sholders Edgor has som
cough yet dan shelton is
down in his back with the
reumitsom I hope you all
gitting along all right did
you git home safe We had a
right nice tim While you Was
up christmas do you thing
you Will git up in march
John Was up here sunday

(Letter written by Marinda Hughes Simpson)

Jan The 11 he just staid over sunday & went back Well I have no nesbs to tell you this tim & maby more the next tim Well I will clos address Laffrenel Kansas r r No 9 Bot 36 your mother marinda Simpson

Figure 1Mariah Harris Proctor

(1871-1965)

The daughter of James Harris and Rachel Doss. She was the inspiration for my poem, "Grandmother." She often spoke of being raised by her grandparents, James and Luseni Doss, former slaves who became landowners and philanthropist in Louisiana.

THE WAR IN KOSOVO, THE US CIVIL WAR, AND THE CAUSE FOR DIVERSITY
BY LINDA HUGHES-DORAME

TODAY, WE OFTEN HEAR OF THE WAR IN KOSOVO AND NOW OF THE COUNTRY'S OCCUPATION BY NATO AND RUSSIAN TROOPS TO RESTORE PEACE, ESTABLISH RECONSTRUCTION, AND HELP SERBS AND ALBANIANS LIVE TOGETHER. WHAT IS HAPPENING THERE REMINDS US OF THE CIVIL WAR IN THIS COUNTRY, THE OCCUPATION OF FEDERAL TROOPS AND THE ERA OF RECONSTRUCTION IN THE SOUTH. I AM, FIRST OF ALL, PROUD TO SAY THAT MY OWN ANCESTOR, JOSEPH SIMPSON, SERVED IN THE 65TH UNITED STATES COLORED INFANTRY.

MY GREAT GRANDMOTHER, BORN TO IN 1871, OFTEN COMMENTED ABOUT THE FAILURE OF

RECONSTRUCTION EFFORTS IN THE SOUTH. THIS FAILURE WAS DUE TO THE LACK OF EDUCATION AMONG THE FORMER SLAVES AND THE DISUNITY THAT EXISTED AMONG AND BETWEEN ALL GROUPS IN THE POPULATION. HOPEFULLY, THE PEACE-KEEPIN TROOPS AND PEOPLE OF KOSOVO WILL BE MORE SUCCESSFUL. IN BOTH CONFLICTS, THE ROOT CAUSES CAN BE TRACED TO A MISUNDERSTANDING AND INTOLERANCE TO THOSE SHO SOMEHOW DIFFER.

THE BLACK CIVIL WAR SOLDIER WAS FIGHTING NOT ONLY FOR HIS COUNTRY, BUT ALSO HIS LIFE AND THE LIVES OF HIS FAMILY. MANY OF THESE SOLDIERS LOST THEIR LIVES IN THE STRUGGLE AS THEY EXPRESSED A WILLINGNESS TO GIVE THEIR LIVES RATHER THAN BE SLAVES.

AT THE BEGINNING OF THE WAR, BLACKS WERE NOT ALLOWED TO FIGHT IN WHAT WAS CALLED A "WHITE

MAN'S WAR." HOWEVER, EVENTUALLY THEY WERE ALLOWED TO FIGHT AFTER THE INSISTENCE OF SUCH PERSONS AS GEOPGE FREDERICK DOUGLAS AND NORTHERN WHITES, SOME WHO WERE MORE CONCERNED WITH HAVING THEM SUBSTITUTE FOR WHITE SOLDIERS. THEY PROVED TO BE REMARKABLE SOLDIERS AND SOME WON THE CONGRESSIONAL MEDAL OF HONOR. THE BRAVERY AND GALLANTRY OF THE MASSACHUSETTS 54TH COLORED INFANTRY BECAME FAMILIAR TO MILLIONS AROUND THE WORLD WITH THE RELEASE OF THE MOVIE, "GLORY." THESE SOLDIERS TIPPED THE BALANCE FOR THE UNION.

WHEN THE WAR ENDED, BLACK SOLDIERS WERE TOLD BY THEIR WHITE COMMANDING OFFICERS TO RETURN TO THEIR HOMES AND THE COUNTRY WAS NOW AS MUCH THEIRS AS IT WAS THEIRS. BUT ONE HUNDRED YEARS WOULD PASS BEFORE THE SEEDS PLANTED BY

THE UNION VICTORY AND THE END OF SLAVERY WOULD COME TO FRUITION IN AMERICAN LIFE. ONE HUNDRED YEARS LATER, AFRICAN AMERICANS AND THEIR WHITE ALLIES IN THE CIVIL RIGHTS MOVEMENT WITH GREAT COURAGE WOULD CAUSE THE PASSAGE OF A SERIES OF CIVIL RIGHTS LAWS THAT GUARANTEED FULL AND EQUAL RIGHTS FOR AF RICAN AMERICANS AS WELL AS WOMEN AND MEMBERS OF OTHER MINORITY GROUPS.

HOWEVER THE STRUGGLE STILL CONTINUES IN THE BATTLE FOR EQUALITY AND DIVERSITY. DR. MARTIN LUTHER KING REMINDED US THAT WE MUST ALWAYS HAVE FAITH AND IN HIS "I HAVE A DREAM SPEECH," ELOQUENTLY STATED THAT WITH FAITH, "WE WILL BE ABLE TO TRANSFORM THE JANGLING DISCORDS OF OUR NATION INTO A BEAUTIFUL SYMPHONY OF BROHTERHOOD."

I, ADRIAN, ALSO FEEL THAT WE SHOULD PRAY FOR THE PEOPLE LIVING IN KOSOVO WHO ARE LIVING IN A WAR STRUCK COUNTRY. WE SHOULD ALSO PRAY FOR OURSELVES WHO ARE LIVING IN A COUNTRY WHERE THERE IS STILL SOME INTOLERANCE AND SCHOOL SHOOTINGS.

MY SON, ADRIAN HUGHES-DORAME, DELIVERED THIS SPEECH ON JUNE 19, 1999 BEFORE A SMALL CHUCH GATEHERING IN OBSERVANCE OF THE JUNETEENTH CELEBRATION.

Linda Hughes-Dorame

Bibliography

HAWKINS, ANNE P. W. "HOEING THEIR OWN ROW, BLACK AGRICULTURE AND THE AGARIAN IDEA IN KANSAS, 1880-1920." KANSAS HISTORY, VOLUME 22, NO. 3, AUTUMN 1999.

HIGGINSON, THOMAS W. "ARMY LIFE IN A BLACK REGIMENT," NEW YORK: PENGUIN PUTNAM INC, 1997.

PARKER, MARTHA AND LAIRD, BETTY, "SOIL OF OUR SOULS, HISTORIES OF THE CLINTON LAKE AREA COMMUNITIES." OVERTON: PARKER-LAIRD ENTERPRISES 1994,

PARKER, MARTHA J. "ANGELS OF FREEDOM," EDITED BY CHRISTINE REINHARD 1999.

TAYLOR, SUSIE K., "A BLACK WOMAN'S CIVIL WAR MEMOIRS," BOSTON: TAYLOR 1902.

Linda Hughes-Dorame

About the authors

LINDA HUGHES-DORAME

LINDA HUGHES-DORAME IS A FREE-LANCE WRITER, SHE HOLDS A MASTER'S DEGREE FROM THE UNIVERSITY OF OKLAHOMA. SHE IS MARRIED AND THE MOTHER OF TWO TEENAGERS, AGES 13 AND 16. SHE ENJOYS WRITING

BECAUSE IT ALLOWS SELF-EXPRESSION IN WORDS YOU WON'T SAY IN NORMAL CONVERATION. HER OTHER HOBBIES INCLUDE TRAVELLING AND COLLECTING DOLLS AND ARTIFACTS.

MARIA HUGHES-DORAME

IS A 7TH GRADE STUDENT, SHE HAS BEEN WRITING SINCE SHE WAS VERY YOUNG. SHE SAID SHE ENJOYS WRITING BECAUSE IT IS A WAY FOR HER TO EXPRESS

HERSELF. SHE ALSO ENJOYS MUSIC AND TRAINING HER
DOGS.

FRANCES A. HENDERSON

FRANCES HENDERSON ATTENDED SOUTHWESTERN
COLLEGE IN OKLAHOMA CITY. SHE WRITES
OCCASIONALLY, BUT MAINLY ENJOYS LISTENING TO
GOSEPEL MUSIC, READING, AND SEWING. SHE HAS
EXPERIENCE DRIVING SCHOOL BUSES.

Linda Hughes-Dorame

Figure 2Maria Hughes-Dorame

Printed in the United States
813800002B

9 781403 334541